D0586269

The Old-Timers' Guide to Life

summersdale

THE OLD-TIMERS' GUIDE TO LIFE

Text abridged from *The Deranged Book for Old-Timers*, first published in 2008 by Summersdale Publishers Ltd

This edition published 2011

This edition copyright © Marcus Waring, 2011

The right of Marcus Waring to be identified as the author of this work has been asserted in accordance with sections 77 and 78 of the Copyright, Designs and Patents Act 1988.

Illustrations by Ian Baker

All rights reserved.

No part of this book may be reproduced by any means, nor transmitted, nor translated into a machine language, without the written permission of the publishers.

Condition of Sale
This book is sold subject to the condition that it shall not, by way of trade or otherwise, be lent, re-sold, hired out or otherwise circulated in any form of binding or cover other than that in which it is published and without a similar condition including this condition being imposed on the subsequent publisher.

Summersdale Publishers Ltd
46 West Street
Chichester
West Sussex
PO19 1RP
UK

www.summersdale.com

Printed and bound in China

ISBN: 978-1-84953-177-1

Substantial discounts on bulk quantities of Summersdale books are available to corporations, professional associations and other organisations. For details contact Summersdale Publishers by telephone: +44 (0) 1243 771107, fax: +44 (0) 1243 786300 or email: nicky@summersdale.com.

The Old-Timers' Guide to Life

Marcus Waring
Illustrations by Ian Baker

INTRODUCTION

There goes Father Time again. With his dodgy back and long-handled scythe, which has Health and Safety reaching for their clipboards, this wizened figure lurks backstage, until the day comes when you hit 60, look in the mirror and realise you are officially an old-timer. In your thirties and forties, you might have thought the clock was racing, but now it seems to be using banned substances as well, and getting on in life brings change.

The Old-Timers' Guide to Life seeks to find those other, more sedated pleasures, from exploring the afternoon snooze to how to twitch curtains properly. It is time to blow a raspberry at Death, and give Father Time a firm kick up the bum. Yes, we are going to grow old, but we are going to make sure we do it disgracefully.

ESSENTIAL CLUTTER

When you were young, you wouldn't have dreamt of disappearing into the woods for a day of derring-do without childhood essentials such as: a penknife, three marbles and a rhubarb and custard chew (with bits of fluff stuck to it). The canny old-timer also knows there are certain things that are essential to help you get through the day.

Reading glasses

Having a pair of glasses to hand becomes vital if you want to see what you are reading. Getting chains so you can hang the glasses round your neck is a fine idea, but with the drawback of catching half your lunch in them – although this can be a nice surprise when you are doing the crossword and become peckish at around 4 p.m.

Tissues

Tissues are hugely important. Your grandchildren will be amazed at the seemingly inexhaustible supply, and they will go wide-eyed with a mixture of surprise and horror when a used one falls out onto the table during Sunday lunch. Remember to always keep your sleeves adequately loaded.

Walking stick

The stick can lend you an air of authority when pointing to things, especially when being asked directions by strangers. Arguably their finest use came into being when some ingenious fellow hollowed out a compartment near the top and installed a sneaky little flask of alcohol, which became known as a tippler.

Try this: the crook of a walking stick is very useful for picking up things like dogs or small children.

THE GREY MATTERS

Once you have partially or totally retired, you have a lot of time on your hands – sometimes too much. The irony is dreadful – you spend your working life looking forward to retirement, only to lose the plot and fall to bits when you get there. So find yourself a few stimulating hobbies to keep your mind busy.

Doing the crossword

A version of a crossword has been found inscribed on an ancient tomb in Egypt. One down's clue was 'A collection of locusts, sounds a bit like vague', and the answer was 'plague' – they had weeks of laughter with that. Then someone got carried away with 'A female ruler with really bad teeth', Queen Hatshepsut got to hear of this and everything went horribly wrong for someone.

Difficult words:

Azimuth – an angular distance measured along a horizon of an object from north or south points. We knew that.

Fanfaronade – boasting, or a blast of trumpets. This is common in gentlemen's toilets.

Wayzgoose – the company 'do', such as a dinner, typically used among printing firms. Why call it the office piss-up when you can get geese involved?

Scrabble

There is nothing like a good game of Scrabble when you are feeling wild, especially when it is accompanied by hot cocoa. The highest recorded score was by a carpenter in Massachusetts called Michael Cresta in 2006, who accumulated 830 points. Words you should keep in mind next time you play include:

Quixotic – extravagantly chivalrous or generous – except when losing at Scrabble.

Squeezy – like your loved one after too much nougat.

Crypt – a space below a church where you might have ended up being stored in olden times.

Psst – a noise you make to get someone's attention. Or a slow fart. Both can have the same effect but the response varies.

KEEP ON TRUCKING

If the idea of retirement has you reaching for the panic button, simply don't retire. You will be financially better off than many of your peers and you will keep mind and body stimulated and entertained. Just don't turn up for an interview with string holding up your trousers.

Jobs that laugh in the face of ageism

Porn star

Forget those honed and toned slim young things banging away at each other – the emerging market is letting it all hang out, wrinkles and all. Storylines can also involve completely new angles. Where once a slim blonde gets the plumber round, now it's all about having your bus pass revoked for bad behaviour on the number 57, and having to go down to the local council office for a good spanking.

Acting extras

You are mature enough not to care what the casting director thinks of your love handles, and you had to stop that cocaine habit years ago due to a dicky heart. You might not get paid very well, and will do hours of standing about, but the hot drinks are on tap and the scope for pointless chit-chat is endless. The best way to get in on the action is to find an agent or ring the producer and cajole them until their ears bleed.

Charity shop assistant

OK, so it doesn't pay the bills, but you get first dibs on any items you want to snaffle for yourself and it bolsters your odds for getting into heaven. The downside is you have to rifle through bags of rags reeking of mothballs and try to play Connect Four with Monopoly pieces on quiet days.

FORTY WINKS

A six-year Greek study recently concluded that regular siestas reduce your chances of dying of heart disease by 34 per cent. Across the Mediterranean, low instances of heart disease are associated with a daily lie-down, although it has also been said that in France the siesta is just an elaborate excuse for a bit of nooky, which also helps keep you perky. Bear in mind that whoever coined the phrase 'You snooze, you lose' was a complete idiot.

The best of the rest

The afternoon doze

This is a classic entry-level nap for beginners – tactics range from donning an airline eye-mask and just passing out in your chair to a full-blown sleep in bed.

Evening television

Maybe it is because the other half wants to watch Alan Titchmarsh molesting some seagulls but, belly swelled with supper, all those exciting nuggets you highlighted in the *Radio Times* are soon distant trivialities in the land of nod.

The summer hammock

If you have a garden and some conveniently placed trees, hang up a hammock. It might be the only sort of swinging you do these days, but it's germ-free and easier on the knees.

PIMP YOUR RIDE

Many of us have heard music blaring, tyres screeching, and girls, with nothing but excessive drinking and cheap sex on their minds, shrieking their heads off on a Saturday night – and that's just down at the local Women's Institute. Boy racers congregating in car parks to talk alloys and burn some rubber has become a national pastime. It's time to fight fire with fire and reclaim the streets with your customised electric scooter – just remember to indicate sensibly.

Get the look

1. Get a white baseball cap – most high-street sports shops can help.

2. Have a cigarette hanging from your mouth – ignore the health implications. Who cares at your age? Image is everything.

3. Invest in a scooter cape – a magnificent waterproof sheet for draping over you and your machine in adverse weather conditions. However, it is a huge fire hazard with that dangling cigarette, and your new boy racer friends won't want to hang out with a giant condom on four pram wheels – think pimp, not blimp.

FASHION

You know you are approaching the autumnal era when you are receiving hand-me-ups instead of hand-me-downs, as your fashion-savvy children take pity on your ailing wardrobe. Charity shops remain a good source of raiment on the cheap, but you don't want to be the scruffy one at the bus stop with the holey shoes that are more pavement than patent.

Hair today, gone tomorrow

There are a few hairstyles to choose from as you age...

Totally bald

A simple and total reduction means you save about an hour a day on messing about in front of the mirror. Use this extra time to heckle the Salvation Army Band in the local shopping centre when they get a note wrong instead.

The comb-over

Accompanied by a soft soundtrack of sniggering and pointing wherever it goes, if your old friend Bob starts turning up at the working men's club with one of these, for pity's sake tell him to behave and cut it off.

The bouffant

Using back-combing and hair spray, you can soon have the coiffured allure of Hyacinth Bucket from *Keeping up Appearances* or the steely persona of Margaret Thatcher. Kim Jong-il, the not so 'Dear Leader' of North Korea, might be a brute but he's got a comical version of this hairstyle.

BALD

COMB-OVER

BOUFFANT

Wonderwear

Look in the back of any national magazine or paper and you will find thousands of adverts for the kind of women's underwear that, at first glance, might be something skydivers would use to safely reach the ground. Young people are at once fascinated and terrified by these alien adverts for unseen garments. What does this strap do? Where does that go? And why is it all so large? Don't worry – they will understand some day.

Footwear

Sensible shoes

This is the border-crossing where fashion is handed over in exchange for practicality. You might not look very sexy but you will be steady on your feet in adverse conditions.

Sandals

Rumour has it that these were first called Jesus sandals after someone shouted 'Jesus! Look at those awful sandals'. You will look like a Geography teacher, although they will allow your stifled trotters to breathe more easily.

ENTERTAINMENT

Whether it's vehemently defending your pruning techniques or wondering who you can ring up and shout at, stave off boredom by going out and seizing the world by the scruff of its neck. Or stay at home and peer at the neighbours through your net curtains. The good thing about seniority is nobody can tell you what to do.

How to get on the *Antiques Roadshow*

Your other half has found a chipped vase in a box in the attic and suddenly everyone is avidly discussing the Ming Dynasty around the house. Talk soon turns to getting on the *Antiques Roadshow*. You never know – that typewriter from the 1920s you picked up at the car boot sale might just pay for several new hips.

Three ways to beat the *Antiques Roadshow* queues:

1. Sleep overnight in the car to be first in line. People already do this so you have to clandestinely superglue their car doors shut in the dead of night to beat the morning rush.

2. Study blueprints of the location and try to infiltrate the perimeter through the sewage system. People with Special Forces training are most suited to this.

3. Borrow a paramedic's uniform and a wheelchair and wheel a friend in, saying they can't stand in queues as they suffer from gerascophobia (a fear of growing old).

A guide to curtain-twitching

The best way to safely observe events in your street is through a sturdy pair of net curtains and with a good, steady wrist. The key to really successful twitching is to subtly let the neighbours know you saw every bit of their blazing row. But remember– a sudden wrong twitch at a critical juncture could well result in a brick through the window and your hand–curtain coordination would be damaged for weeks.

Rumour-spreading for beginners

As things slow down in your own scandal department, it's time to start rummaging about in other people's. A verbal equivalent of curtain twitching, some top lines for getting a bit of trouble on the boil and keeping yourself entertained are:

' And I couldn't help noticing that Trevor from number fifty-six was putting what looked like a body in the boot of his car on Friday night. '

' Well that's odd. She told me she hated Gladys's collection of humorous tea towels. '

' And you'll never guess who I saw buying condoms in Boots this morning – ribbed ones too. '

Knitting

When you grow bored of making scarves, five alternative uses for knitting needles are:

1. Cleaning your ears (carefully)

2. Poking trick-or-treaters through the letterbox

3. Performing affordable acupuncture on people you don't really like

4. Skewering the neighbour's cat after it peed in your pansies

5. Skewering the neighbour after they fail to grasp the importance of the pansies

STRIKING UP CONVERSATIONS WITH COMPLETE STRANGERS

Old-timers are masters of communication when it comes to talking with strangers. Partly because they are from a forgotten age when people were nice to each other and partly because they only have a budgerigar to talk to at home. Classic settings for striking up conversations are...

The bus stop

Start cautiously with an enquiry about the route/time/bus number/ when the last bus came through. If your chosen conversationalist seems interested, move onto recent bus journeys (delays and mishaps are always popular topics) and then go for the heavier subjects, including the price of the bus and how the new seats are gentler on one's bottom.

Talking about the weather

If it's pouring with rain this tends to start a conversation off gloomily but then it can either descend into outright complaining, which is always popular, or to 'Oh well, mustn't grumble', and further opportunities to show that you are an optimist. This can be especially useful if you fancy the person you are discussing global warming with.

Minding your peas and queues

When standing in a supermarket queue, conversation can range from nutritional topics to what kind of loo paper is on a 'two for one' deal. Do note that talking so much that you are completely unprepared when the time comes to pay goes down very badly, especially when it's Saturday and working professionals in their thirties and forties are wondering why you couldn't have done all your shopping during the week.

GARDENING

A much-needed breath of fresh air, not only is it a wonderful way of getting outdoors and giving yourself a dose of oxygen, but you can also burn 350 calories in an hour, which is handy if the only thing you are currently growing is fat.

A Gardener's Paradise

Topiary

Bring out the inner artist and turn any large bushes into peacocks and random marsupials. If, after hours of careful clipping and shaping, you are left with a vague blob that looks like a badly savaged shrub instead of a leaping ferret, give in to the rising anger and take a sharp axe to your unhelpful creation.

Ornamental ponds

As well as providing a haven for newts, toads and cigarette butts, a nice little pond is perfect for unsuspecting animals to drown in, or as a nursery for thousands of mosquitoes, which will rise up in clouds and drain everyone of their thin and precious blood.

Allotments

Allotments really took off in the nineteenth century when Victorians in cities were encouraged to steer their activities away from getting pissed and falling in the gutter. Bear this in mind as you gather a few friends together to drink ginger wine and end up face down in the cabbages.

OLD SPORT

If shearing and pruning in the garden is not enough excitement for you, burn some calories playing sport. It's less hassle than sex and there is a better chance of victory at the end of it.

Bowls

Favoured by the elderly because you can be as unhealthy as a packet of pork scratchings but still become a champion, it's a kind of relaxation therapy with lots of grass – similar to the sixties, but different. If you are male, do not be put off by the ladies flashing a bit of calf as they bowl in those racy pleated skirts. The saucy minxes are just trying to distract you.

Old spokes' home

Cycling is a really great way of combating heart disease, diabetes, obesity and other exciting side-effects of sitting on your bum all day wondering where the time goes. It's also gentle on your hips, knees and joints. Running might be great for fun and fitness but it can wear out your knees more quickly than sex on wooden floorboards.

Cycling glossary:

Break wind – this is cycling so that another cyclist can follow in your slipstream. If you were thinking of something else, get your mind out of the gutter.

Granny gear – the lowest gear available. We find this derogatory in the extreme and will be writing to the relevant organisations to get this phrase changed to 'Age-challenged chain setting'.

Tandem – the only people in society who can get away with riding the two-person bicycle are old or tossers. Triumph in being the former and blaze off into the sunset, while muttering about the person behind not pulling their weight.

Fishing

There is nothing more relaxing than dangling your worm in the water while not thinking of anything – except maybe fishing.

Three fish you don't want to catch:

1. The great white shark – if you hook one of these down at the local pond, you are buggered. Growing to around 24 feet and weighing over 3 tons, it will yank you into the water and blend you into a pink cloud in seconds.

2. The box jellyfish – if you plan to go fishing in Australia, try not to catch one of these highly venomous and squidgy beasts. And don't put it on your head and pretend it's a humorous Halloween mask to your fishing buddies.

3. The shopping trolley – these are more common in UK waters. Full-grown trolleys have been known to fight for hours before they can be reeled in, testing the stamina and skill of the fisherman to the extreme.

TRAVEL

Y ou may have lots more boxes to tick on the travel insurance forms nowadays, and there is a sneaking feeling that when you conk out halfway up Kilimanjaro, the swines are going to leave you there for the hyenas. But plough on regardless – travel is food for the soul; it just needs to be mashed up by someone nice in a uniform now.

The coach trip

Like the bus but hijacked specially by the elderly, often for day trips to places that sell postcards and cream teas. These trips are not to be confused with National Express coaches, where delights can include drunken football fans fighting at the back and the coach pulling into every insignificant dot of civilisation on long journeys.

Cruises

OK, so the *Titanic* didn't go strictly according to plan, but it was memorable. Things have improved since the old days – the only major danger now is getting stuck with that really dull couple from Widnes for the entire trip or catching a dose of virulent food poisoning, which seems to sweep through cruise ships more often than the cleaners.

Useful phrases for old-timers abroad

Norwegian
'Reisekameraten min har falt overbord i fjorden.'
'My travelling companion has fallen overboard into the fjord.'

Hebrew

'Hakadurim hakhadashim hae'le beshvil halev memal'im oti bekhayim.'

'These new heart pills are making me frisky.'

French

'J'ai peut être l'air crevé mais je carbure total.'

'I might look knackered but I still go like a train.'

Russian

'Shto utziba yest shto likhko jzewat?'

'What do you have that is easy to chew?'

SAVE A PRETTY PENNY

Face it – life is getting more and more expensive. If you have been a foolish thing and failed to stash enough money away, don't panic. Just because they have cut the gas off and debt collectors are readying the removals van, you can save money in unexpected areas.

Wheels and deals

The bus pass

The free bus pass will land on the mat when you turn 60. Cheer yourself with reaching this milestone by joyriding at low speeds into town to wander aimlessly, get in people's way and waste shop assistants' time by asking them to demonstrate how things that you have no intention of buying work.

Supermarket coupons

Not exactly as exciting as jumping out of an aeroplane, but the rush you get when you receive a free jar of beetroot is reasonably special.

Rootle

The OAP who has blown the monthly allowance on a comical letter-opener or hand-engraved backscratcher can save a tidy sum with what Mother Nature provides in the giant larder that is the countryside.

Plants

Sloes, which can be picked in September and October, are used to make winter-warming sloe gin, which will have you drunk in minutes. And there is absolutely nothing wrong with setting up camp next to an apple tree and brewing your own cider while living rough for a couple of days.

Fungi

Oyster mushrooms might cost a bomb at a local market but they are probably sprouting for free just up the road. Just make sure you carry a book to avoid picking poisonous mushrooms and going wheels up after making quiche using the cheerfully named 'destroying angel'.

Animals

Road kill, if still warm, can be good. Pheasants, deer and badgers are all edible, and with practice you will soon be exploring the delights of pigeon tikka masala.

Things you can burn for fuel

1. **Your spouse** – when they pop their clogs, this can save a fortune on cremation fees and really cuts down on red tape. It will also keep the house warm for a couple of days, but maybe save those marshmallows for another time – dignity and all that.

2. **The net curtains** – your style rating will improve but they will give off little heat and, if you have done a lot of frying over the years, they may go up rather suddenly.

3. **Your entire collection of *Steam Railway Magazine.***

FOOD AND DRINK

As you begin to no longer feel like the sharpest tool in the box, stave off going a bit gaga with a powerful mix of intelligent foodstuffs. And then undo all the good work with some mind-bending traditional cocktails.

Brain food

Coffee

Those boffins in white coats in the US have decided that a cup of coffee a day might help prevent Alzheimer's. Drink too much full-strength Colombian, however, and you will get the shakes anyway.

Oily fish

Generally good for the mind, but with the added boost that iodine is wonderful for a bit of mental clarity. After a few weeks, you might be standing next to the sardines in the supermarket and for once not staring into space thinking 'Now what did I come here for?'

Nuts

Good for energy and can stave off depression and elevate the mood. Be careful telling partners about your fondness for Brazilians – they might start pouring hot wax on your nether regions.

A little tipple

Then you can undo all the virtuous self-denial of the above with these old-fashioned drinks with a touch of class. Put out the cat and have a cocktail party at home – you will be in the recovery position for days.

The Old-Fashioned

It's got your name written all over it. Cole Porter penned a song called 'Make it Another Old-fashioned, Please', and at one time it was known as the 'palate-paralyser', which has a warning in there somewhere.

Ingredients:
2 measures of bourbon
A dash of Angostura bitters
1 sugar cube
Soda water

Method – place a sugar cube in an Old-Fashioned glass (it's like a big tumbler) and soak with the Angostura bitters. Add enough soda to cover the sugar cube and crush it using a spoon. Add the bourbon and top up with soda. Give it all a stir and finish with a slice of orange and a maraschino cherry. Drop a twist of lemon in the drink and stand well back.

The sidecar

This surfaced in the early part of the twentieth century and is rumoured to have been invented by Harry from Harry's Bar in Paris, where it was created for an army captain who was driven to the bar in a motorcycle sidecar. The name might have also come from the fact that if you had too many, there was no way you were going to be the one riding the motorbike.

Ingredients:
1 part brandy
1 part Triple Sec
1 part lemon or lime juice

Method – fill a shaker with ice, put everything in together, give it a good shake and strain into a cocktail glass.

PETS CORNERED

Studies have shown that pets have a positive effect on mood and well-being as well as keeping you physically active. They also offer companionship and loyalty, give your day some routine and they don't disappear down the pub for hours while spending the housekeeping on double vodkas.

Pets that aren't a total nuisance

Dogs

They can be lively but this means that they can also be noisy and hence a complete pain. Don't forget how useful the dog can be for fetching slippers – and dog-walking is a great euphemism for a nip to the pub.

Cats

Moody, self-indulgent and they use the flowerbed as a toilet. Unlike a dog, a cat will not recycle the newspaper before you have read it, and will quickly fit in with your routine of not doing very much all day long. Note that they are a waste of money if confronted by a burglar. They will simply flirt outrageously and ask to be fed.

Tortoises

Not one for the thrill-seeking adrenaline addict, but a solid, dependable companion until it wanders off through the hedge and is never seen again. Note that if you can't keep up with your pet tortoise walking round the garden you really are past it.

Pets that might not be such a great idea

Elephants

Male African elephants can grow to 12 feet tall and weigh around 15,000 lb. This has got 'Pensioner Flattened in Jumbo Horror' written all over it.

Tigers

Tiger cubs might be little cuties to romp around with in the garden, but one day when they are bigger one of them will get carried away and sink its 5-inch claws into your back and it will all go pear-shaped. If you insist on getting one, keeping it in the shed on your allotment will guarantee nobody fools with your prized cucumbers again.

Lobsters

It takes seven years for a lobster to reach a weight of approximately 1 lb. It takes seven seconds to say 'lobster thermidor' really slowly. One day there is bound to be a conflict of interest and horrid scenes involving boiling water.

LET'S GET PHYSICAL

There's nothing more exciting than having a good conversation about your maladies, and as the years fall by more and more falls off, giving you plenty of subject matter. There are a range of health issues to consider and any one could affect you.

DIY anti-wrinkle cream

A wrinkle is a crease on the surface of the skin. It's also a sign of ageing that nobody wants. You could spend a fortune on complicated lotions and potions full of exciting things nobody has ever heard of, or try the following inappropriate alternatives:

Animal fat

Roman women used refined animal fats in their face cream. You might smell like yesterday's bacon but your skin will be baby-smooth.

Mayonnaise

Forget chicken sandwiches – rubbing a bit of mayonnaise into your face at night works a treat. Also for the dog, who will lick you awake with more enthusiasm than normal.

Emu oil

Made from the refined fats of emus, this has been used by the Aborigines in Australia for thousands of years. To keep costs down, you will have to poach some emus from a local farm and process their fat yourself, which could be dangerous and wreak havoc with your shoes.

The Little Blue Pill

Taking a dose of Viagra is all fine and large, but do be aware that, in rare cases, erections can last for more than four hours. This could well be three hours and 55 minutes too long for a lot of people. A small number of people have also experienced a sudden loss of vision, but this can be handy if you are having sex with someone who isn't exactly an oil painting.

How to put people off their food

If you are in a crowded restaurant, hospital or at a busy family dinner, there are several ways to put people off their food and double your calorific intake at no extra cost. Favourites include:

6 They said they had never seen a tapeworm that long. Actually it looked a bit like your tagliatelle. 9

6 I always forget to wash my hands after going to the loo. My genital warts medication makes me forgetful. Bread rolls, anyone? They're still warm. 9

6 The first thing I wanted to eat in hospital after they operated on my piles was meatballs. Don't ask me why. 9

DEATH - DEAL WITH IT

Possibly the most worrying thing about time is that one day you, me and that annoying man who couldn't remember his PIN number in the newsagent this morning will all be dead. Death levels all with his sharpened sickle and stand-up comedy routine. You should see his impression of Joan Rivers; it'll kill you.

Be different

We all know the usual ways of shuffling off this mortal coil, from heart attacks to watching party political broadcasts until your brain leaks out of your nose. But if you want to stand out from the herd, opt for the departure with a difference.

Plane crash

You have to be something of a rarity to peg it in a plane crash. It is nearly as hard as enjoying the food. Go and sit at the front, but not too close to the doors, and distract the pilots if on a small craft with relaxed security.

Lightning

It's funny stuff, lightning – unless you happen to get hit by it. Odds vary but it's around a one in three million chance. If you are sweaty or rain-soaked and are struck by lightning, the water can turn to steam, sometimes causing your shoes and clothes to be blown off. Golfers are statistically the most at risk, which is quite handy as losing their clothes and shoes would make the average golfer less of a weeping sore on the face of fashion.

Top funeral songs

1. 'Highway to Hell' by AC/DC will not only give the vicar a fright, but the audience will be put in mind of a man in a schoolboy's shorts and cap playing powerful guitar riffs. It could possibly work if you're a lifelong criminal or generally bad person.

2. 'Another One Bites the Dust' by Queen manages to neatly reduce the deceased to a statistic before you can say 'eight-hundred-degree oven'.

3. 'Stayin' Alive' by the Bee Gees – you couldn't and that's why all the teary faces are lining the pews and the worms in the cemetery are going haywire.

KEEP ALIVE (OR KEEP FIT IF YOU ARE AN OPTIMIST)

There are a number of different ways to keep fit as you get older and escape the fatty folds of your favourite chair. Yes, the chair is your friend and is there to support you but if you spend too long in it and not enough outside doing something active, it will come back to bite you on your (now ample) behind.

Exercises for the partially knackered

Nodding your head in time to music

Good for relieving tension in the neck as well as getting a dose of culture and infusing a sense of learning in the house. You may also want to swing or tap a shoe, but don't get carried away.

Washing the dog

This may seem like a trivial exercise but you would be surprised how many calories you will burn giving the pooch a good shampoo, especially if you use conditioner as well. The effort is greatly increased if you have to chase the little so-and-so round the garden for an hour beforehand.

Walking

Nobody is certain why, but old-timers love to walk. Maybe it is because it is gentle on the joints and possibly because it is free.

Self-defence

If you are going to be out and wandering the neighbourhood, you might run into the scourge of the modern age, the hoodie. If you do, it'll pay to have a few moves up your sleeve along with those used tissues:

The 'hoodie' wink

A classic move, all you have to do is distract the hooded assailant for a moment, possibly with a line like 'that old woman over there has just collected her pension'. When he or she looks away, yank the hood down over their head and run for it in the other direction.

The Samson

Just as the great warrior was undone by losing his locks, so the hoodie has an Achilles' heel. Just as the would-be attacker moves in, if his or her hooded top is unzipped, dance nimbly to the left, circle round behind them and in one slick move pull their hooded top off from the back. Their powers will quickly fade and they will slink off in defeat.

Go mobile

Get in close and seize their mobile phone. With their communications shut down, they can't call reinforcements on undersized bicycles and will soon miss listening to their idiotic ringtones so much that they will fall to the ground, weakened to the point of surrender.

OLD SPICE

Is that a bottle of blood pressure pills in your pocket or are you just pleased to see me? Recent research has found that older people who have sex regularly enjoy a superior experience and are mentally and physically better off. There is also evidence that points to people who have more sex living longer. So come and put some kink in your wrinkles.

Zimmer frame *Kama Sutra*

The begonia

Like the lotus position but different. The man sits with his ankles crossed on the floor (put a mat down) and the woman sits on top of him, wrapping her legs around his back. Talking about what plants you should put in the herbaceous borders next spring will get you both in the mood in no time. The Zimmer frame should be left to one side but close to hand in case of severe stiffness. You don't want to have to call for help.

The Twinings

Similar to the twining position, this works well for beginners who are just getting to grips with the *Kama Sutra*. The theory is that you lie on your sides, get entangled and take it from there, basically having a bit of how's-your-father sideways. Keep the Zimmer frame close by and use it to haul yourself up again. Then go and have a lovely pot of assam.

Driving the pig home

Like the position called driving the peg home, but for when the man in the partnership has behaved disgracefully, preferably at a public function like a christening party, and is being driven home by an angry wife who is telling him there will be no hanky panky for a very long time. The Zimmer frame is shut in the boot but can hear every word.

Late dating

You are never too old to get out there and cause a bit of intrigue and scandal while getting the children worried about rash alterations you might make to your will. But there are numerous pitfalls to avoid.

Men

Do say: 'You have great teeth.'
Don't say: 'Where did you buy them?'

Do say: 'Would you like to join me for lunch next Thursday?'
Don't say: 'Can you wear those beige tights that hold the bulges in?'

Women

Do say: 'It's nice to have a man about the house.'
Don't say: 'What do you mean you can't install the Digibox?'

Do say: 'It's very common.'
Don't say: 'I have some horse-strength Viagra at my place.'

FRUIT OF YOUR LOINS

Where would you be without your children? Apart from richer, happier and more relaxed? Yes, they are extraordinarily difficult as babies, but gradually they start to sleep at sensible times, become continent, begin earning their own money and eventually flee the nest, leaving some parents strangely bereft and others quietly popping champagne corks. Do bear in mind that one day, when you have gone mildly loopy, they will be back in charge.

How to cope with...

Christmas

Forget commemorating the birth of Jesus. Christmas is the time when that argument you had over whose fault it was the turkey got burned in 1974 resurfaces. Bad vibes fuelled by alcohol can reach epic proportions, with the added danger that the day is centred around the kitchen, which is full of sharp knives and highly volatile people trying to ignite equally flammable brandy.

Try this: fake a heart attack and then get the ambulance to drop you off at home. Open your rather expensive bottle of Puligny-Montrachet that you were saving for a special occasion and settle down in front of *The Eagle Has Landed*.

Family holidays

Long-haul holidays need careful thought as they have the additional trauma of everyone feeling like they have just landed on the moon and haven't slept since last week. Power-napping on the flight is essential to combat a potential fracas upon arrival.

> **Try this:** 'Accidentally' book yourself into a hotel with a similar name that is several miles in the opposite direction and spend the rest of the holiday actually enjoying yourself.

TECHNOLOGY

Phones have gone from big grey plastic things on the hall table to mobile ones that are small enough to floss your teeth with and can take pictures, play music and run the bath, hopefully not all at once. Almost as hard as understanding what young people are saying or why your pension is almost worthless, technology has moved along quicker than you can say 'Uniform Resource Locator'.

The Internet

Netspeak

If you get into a chatroom conversation with someone more web-savvy, they may bombard you with strange words and acronyms. Avoid trouble by knowing what they are talking about.

A/S/L – age/sex/location
Don't put 'ancient', 'yes please' and 'on the bed'.

GNOC – Get naked on cam
Don't. Unless you are charging them lots of money.

NIFOC – Naked in front of computer
Your computer didn't sign up for this. Do not join them.

TDTM – talk dirty to me
This phrase does not mean they want to know about the time you came in with your walking boots and stamped mud into the shag-pile carpet.

Mobile phones

Even the idiot-proof ones can seem complicated to sexagenarians who are just mastering the dark art of toasting waffles. Sending your first text to your grandchild is a proud moment in any old-timer's book. However, you might want to save your soon-to-be arthritic fingers by using some acronyms.

Text abbreviations for old-timers

iirc – if I remember correctly

irrac – I rarely remember anything correctly

cya– see you later

cyab – see you at bingo

kmt – kiss my teeth

kmtgaptiag – kiss my teeth goodnight and put them in a glass

iwdyiyimasa – I will disinherit you if you interrupt my afternoon snooze again

THE GUIDE TO BEING A GRUMPY CODGER

Make sure you conform to stereotype with the following steps:

1. The frown
Don't you just hate those idiots who tell you it uses 43 muscles to frown and 17 to smile? Tell them your face needs the exercise.

2. The mutter
If someone is getting on your nerves, for example, a person working in a shop, walk off while muttering to yourself in dark tones. You might be using strong words to curse the day they were born or you might just be saying 'rhubarb rhubarb' but it will make you feel a lot better.

3. The tut
A vital tool in your repertoire of disgruntled noises is the humble tut. Strengthen yours using exercises such as rolling your 'r's, licking condensation off windows and always carrying a small bottle of water as a dry mouth can ruin the effectiveness.

Bitching for beginners

Make sure you have got a bit of practice in before you try these ideal subjects in a real-life scenario.

The price of things

Everything is more expensive – don't ever forget that you used to get a haircut for five shillings.

Tax

It's risen. You slaved away for decades doing a job you hated and now you want to vent spleen and tell everyone about it. The plus side is everyone of a working age will agree with you and offer to drive you to London so you can poke the Chancellor in the eye with a sharpened umbrella.

Pensions

The UK has the lowest-value pensions in Europe so you are totally justified in getting fired up over this one. You worked hard for years and now you are having to barbeque the cat and burn the furniture just to stay alive.

Drugs

You can't get hold of really good, strong stuff any more. Bring back the sixties.

FAMOUS LAST WORDS

As we shimmy disgracefully towards the closing of *The Old-Timers' Guide to Life*, the overwhelming desire is to end with something poignant, the suitable full-stop rather than an inadvertent cry of 'Who stole my underpants?' And what more interesting way than perusing the final words of the famous?

'Either that wallpaper goes, or I do.' Oscar Wilde, 1854–1900. Actually called Fingal O'Flahertie Wills, he lived out his days in exile in France and is buried in Père Lachaise cemetery in Paris.

'I am dying. Please… bring me a toothpick.' Alfred Jarry, 1873–1907. The French surrealist writer had a love for the strange.

'I've had a hell of a lot of fun and I've enjoyed every minute of it.' Errol Flynn, 1909–1959. The swashbuckling Australian was rather into the drug-taking, women and booze. No wonder he sounded chipper.

AUTHOR'S LAST WORD

(which is a remote prospect as he never shuts up)

Finally, after getting a bit reflective on life, we reach the end of the journey. Not of life, just this book – where a spot of *Last of the Summer Wine* and a good snooze are the just deserts of the weary reader. The path has been long, risky and occasionally involved swearing, but somehow we have got there in one piece and smelling of blueberries. We have engaged, we have shared and we have seen how to make dangerous cocktails. But most importantly of all, we have learned why we don't keep elephants. May your days be sunny and your taste in pets sensible.

M. W.

www.summersdale.com